EARL THE EARTHWORM
DIGS FOR HIS LIFE

By Tim Magner   Illustrations by Lindsay Knapp

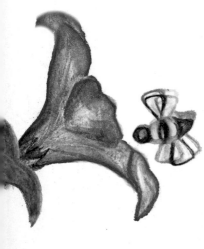

Earl the Earthworm Digs for His Life

Published by Green Sugar Press LLC
Please visit us at: www.greensugarpress.com
Illustrations by Lindsay Knapp
Book Design by Lindsay Knapp
Cover Design by Dallas Drotz
Printed by Service Communication & Solutions (www.swoc.com) on
a mix of post consumer waste recycled paper and
Forest Stewardship Council certified paper.

Publisher's Cataloging-in-Publication data
Magner, Tim.
     Earl the Earthworm Digs for His Life /
     by Tim Magner ; illustrations by Lindsay Knapp.
     p. cm.
     ISBN 978-0-9820417-5-8
     Summary: The coming-of-age age story of an
     earthworm where we learn the connections in
     nature and the environment.

[1. Earthworms–Fiction. 2. Nature–Fiction. 2. Natural history–Fiction.
3. Ecology–Fiction. 4. Earth Sciences–Fiction.] I. Knapp, Lindsay. II. Title.

PZ8.3 .M2724 Ea 2009
[E]--dc22   LCCN: 2008908377

A single, tiny cocoon lay under a leaf in the soil.

Just the size of your thumbnail at birth, most earthworms grow as long as your hand. Certain types in Australia can grow to the size of a car.

3

The cocoon hatches and out pops an earthworm named Earl. Earl the Earthworm explores his surroundings, inching this way and that.

There are 4,400 different types of worms, but all are legless and move by changing from short and stubby to long and skinny.

Earl notices the bumblebees above, buzzing
from flower to flower–no time to linger.
"Wow," imagines Earl, who feels their vibrations.
"I like those wings, how fast they fly!"

Bees are built to pollinate, allowing
flowering plants and trees to grow
seeds. The bee's "buzz" comes from their
wings flapping 200 times per second!

Just then, an army of ants marches by.

There are 10,000 different types of ants. Altogether, ants weigh as much as all the humans on the earth.

Earl crawls along, absorbing the march. "How hard they work," ponders Earl, who realizes he isn't strong like an ant.

The ants march on, leaving Earl behind.

A worker ant can carry ten times its weight.

Now, wild prairie grasses surround Earl,
who understands he is not like the grass either.

*The deep roots of prairie grasses soak up eight
times as much rain as simple wheat or corn plants.*

8

Worse, the blazing sun makes Earl hot and tired.

The sun, a gigantic star 93 million miles away, is the source of all the earth's energy.

Earl continues, wiggling toward darker ground.

Trees cool the plants and anima
beneath their branches and leav
Trees cool themselves by allow.
water to evaporate from their lea

Once in the shade, Earl feels the presence of a towering tree. Probing around its sturdy base, Earl thinks to himself, "This giant must do spectacular things."

Trees provide a home and food to millions of different types of animals.

Traveling around the solid trunk, Earl is more confused and frustrated than ever.

Leaves take in sunlight, water and air to make food for themselves. In the process, trees absorb carbon dioxide and exhale the oxygen we need to breathe.

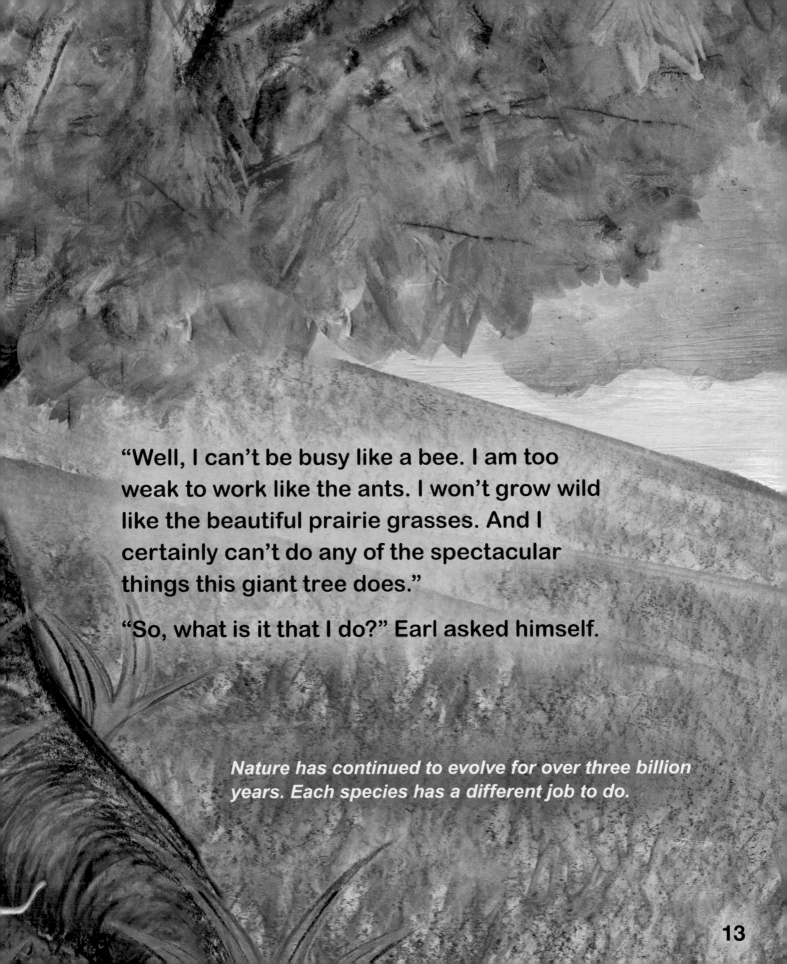

"Well, I can't be busy like a bee. I am too weak to work like the ants. I won't grow wild like the beautiful prairie grasses. And I certainly can't do any of the spectacular things this giant tree does."

"So, what is it that I do?" Earl asked himself.

Nature has continued to evolve for over three billion years. Each species has a different job to do.

13

At just that moment, rain begins to fall from the sky above. Earl can't hear the pitter patter of the rain hitting the ground, but he can feel it.

The rain falls on Earl and all around him.

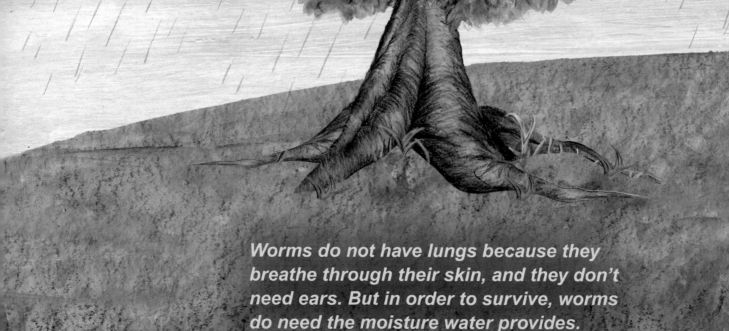

Worms do not have lungs because they breathe through their skin, and they don't need ears. But in order to survive, worms do need the moisture water provides.

As the rainwater gathers, Earl begins to dig,
wriggling and eating his way under the ground.

Why does he dig? Nobody knows for sure, but
if you ask Earl, he'll tell you his gut told him to.

*Even without teeth, worms eat a lot of
leaves and soil. Their gizzard, the stomach,
grinds it all up and breaks it down.*

Earl digs headfirst. And with a body made of muscle, he digs perfectly. He tunnels through the soil, breaking it apart crumb by crumb, even dragging parts of dead leaves with him.

A worm's digging and burrowing keeps the soil loose so it doesn't become hard and useless.

Soon, the water follows Earl down and down, and around, and around.

Worms create useful tunnels that allow air and water to reach below the surface where it is needed.

Suddenly, Earl realizes he isn't alone. In addition to tree and plant roots, an entire miniature zoo inhabits the soil. Tiny creatures too small for us to see with our own eyes, with names like bacteria and fungi, swarm all about.

Weighed together, all the tiny creatures living within the top few inches of the soil are vastly greater than all the animals above the surface of the ground.

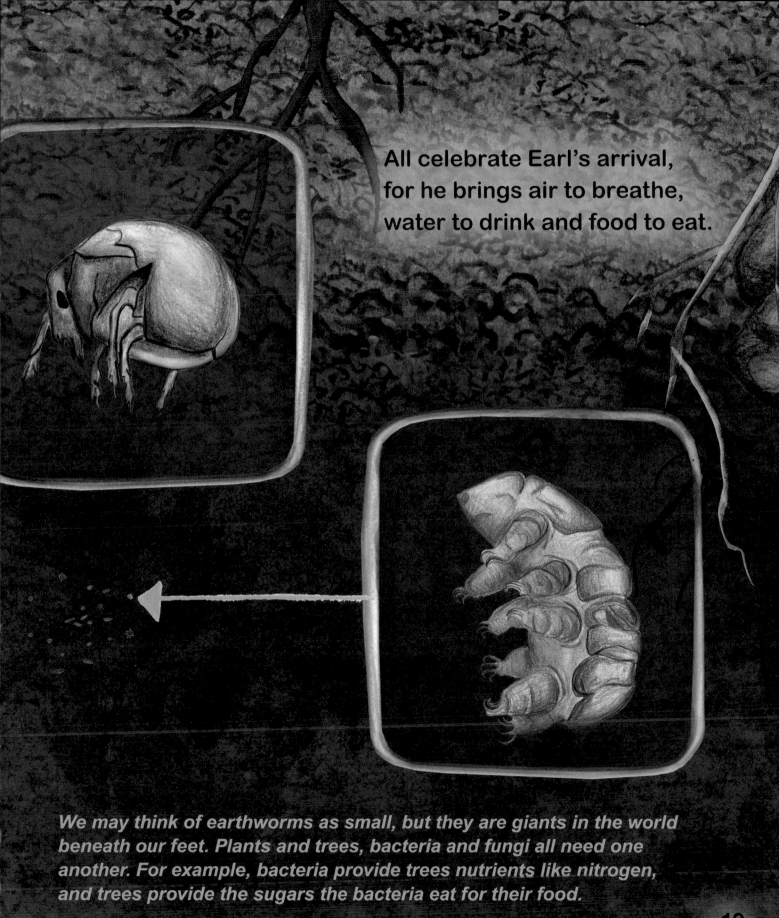

All celebrate Earl's arrival,
for he brings air to breathe,
water to drink and food to eat.

We may think of earthworms as small, but they are giants in the world
beneath our feet. Plants and trees, bacteria and fungi all need one
another. For example, bacteria provide trees nutrients like nitrogen,
and trees provide the sugars the bacteria eat for their food.

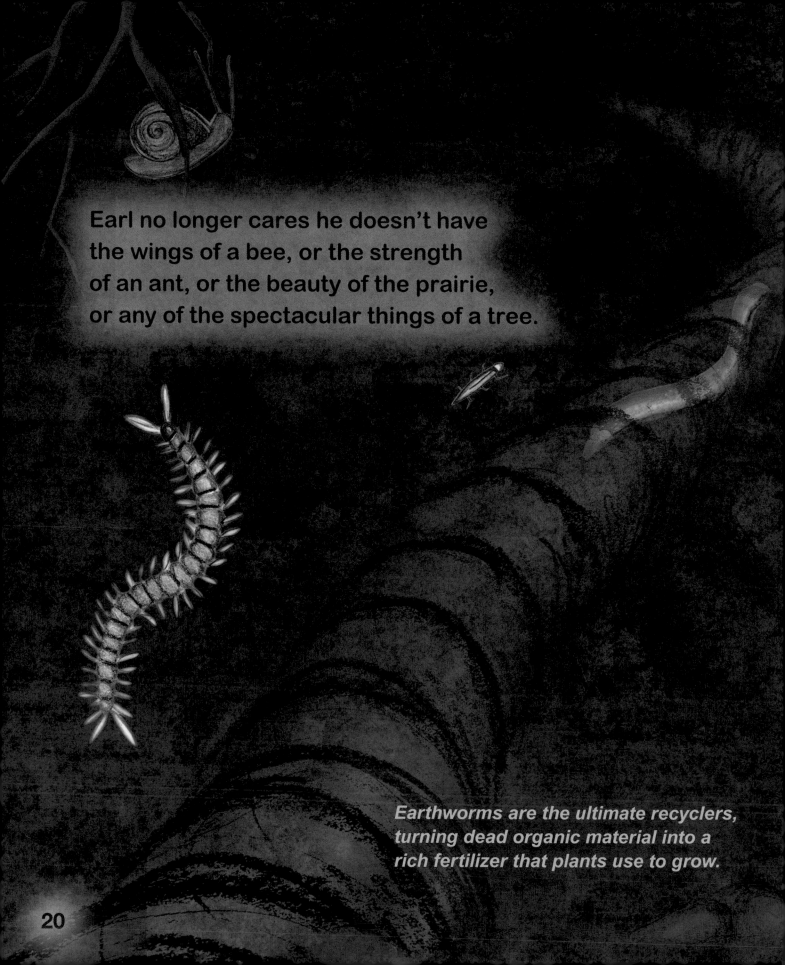

Earl no longer cares he doesn't have
the wings of a bee, or the strength
of an ant, or the beauty of the prairie,
or any of the spectacular things of a tree.

*Earthworms are the ultimate recyclers,
turning dead organic material into a
rich fertilizer that plants use to grow.*

Earl finally understands what he does, and why he does what he does. Everyone and everything connected to Earl's world benefits from his eating and digging.

Gardeners and farmers love earthworms for the good their digging and eating do. Earthworms create healthy soils that benefit flowers, plants, trees and animals

So Earl continued to do what earthworms were made to do: DIG.

And dig Earl did.

Most earthworms have multiple hearts, and all earthworms dig, eat and process dirt and waste. In one year, 16,000 lbs. of soil might pass through the gut of an earthworm!

Earl proudly digs through the damp earth until he reaches the surface. Once on the ground, he deposits the earth's finest fertilizer: his waste.

While Earl can't see like you or me, it doesn't matter. For he can sense:

In an area of healthy soil the size of a football field, there may be over 2,000,000 earthworms.

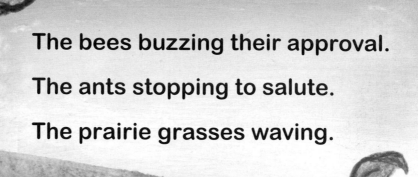

The bees buzzing their approval.

The ants stopping to salute.

The prairie grasses waving.

The labor of bees helps produce 1/3 of the food we eat, including most fruits and vegetables. Ants, like countless other animals, rely on the work of worms to survive and thrive. As we begin to understand the benefits of prairies, we work to replant and restore them.

And perhaps most impressive:

For its friend Earl, the towering tree
sways its trunk and shakes its leaves.

Egyptian Queen Cleopatra declared earthworms must be protected as sacred animals. Aristotle referred to earthworms as "the guts of the soil." In 1881, Charles Darwin wrote about earthworms: "It may be doubted whether there are any animals which have played so important a part in the history of the world, as have these lowly creatures."

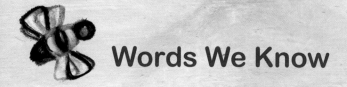

Words We Know

- **Bacteria:** As the first living inhabitants, they make up the vast majority of life on earth. Requiring a microscope to see, as many as 100,000 bacteria might occupy a single inch of land.

- **Carbon:** A basic element and source of energy. Humans and animals breathe in oxygen and exhale carbon. Plants do the reverse.

- **Cocoon:** Where many insects develop and grow before being born.

- **Decompose:** Part of the natural cycle of life. After life, plants and animals die and the decaying process provides food for others and allows for new life.

- **Ecosystem:** An area, such as a forest, lake or prairie, each with its own web of life and community of plants and animals.

- **Invasive Species:** A plant or animal that doesn't belong, or is not native, to a specific area or ecosystem. Transplanting non-native earthworms to an area they don't belong in may cause more damage than good because it disrupts the balance of the ecosystem.

- **Fungi:** Found nearly everywhere, and in countless varieties, such as mushrooms, fungi help break apart dead plants and get them ready for new life.

- **Oligochaetologists:** Scientists who study worms.

- **Photosynthesis:** When bacteria, algae, plants and trees combine energy from the sun with carbon to make food in the form of sugar. This process also produces air for us to breathe.

- **Pollination:** Necessary for flowering plants and trees to produce more seeds. Pollen is often transferred by animals, like bees and birds, between different plants and trees.

Composting with Worms

Earthworms don't have ears, eyes, arms, legs, lungs or bones, but because of their eating habits and how they help enrich the soil, they may be the most valuable animals on earth.

In nature, there is no garbage and there are no landfills. What is waste for one species is food for another species. Composting copies this valuable process and turns our valuable waste into something useful again.

To compost: pile brown waste, like dried leaves, paper, pine needles and hay and layer in green waste like leftover fruit and vegetable scraps, grass clippings and coffee grounds.

Now, add worms. Together, the worms with the soil bacteria and the fungi will dig through and break down the waste and turn it into sweet-smelling compost—a natural fertilizer to help grow big, healthy plants!

Also from Green Sugar Press

*Growing **Green** Minds*

N is for Nature:
An Environmental Alphabet Book

From buzzing bees and gorgeous gorillas, to lovely leafs and wiggling worms, *N is for Nature* excites the eye and inspires the imagination. With simple prose and creative images shaped to form each letter, early readers discover the magic of the alphabet.

An Environmental Guide from A to Z

By examining the elements, habitats and cycles in nature, *An Environmental Guide* introduces basic environmental science to elementary school readers. With a compelling narrative and unforgettable images *An Environmental Guide* brings an awareness of how the world works and encourages kids to explore and connect with nature nearby.

1% For the Planet is a growing global movement of 1,200+ companies that donate 1% of their sales to a network of 1,674 environmental organizations worldwide.